CW01497443

When the Wait Becomes a Weight

The truth about being single,
Waiting on God for marriage

NICOLE C. DIGGS

Copyright © 2016 Nicole C. Diggs

Living Write Books LLC
Lanham, MD

All rights reserved. No part of this book may be reproduced in any form or by any means without the prior written consent of the Publisher, excepting brief quotes used in reviews.

References:

Scripture quotations marked NLT are taken from the *Holy Bible,* New Living Translation, copyright 1996, 2004, 2007 by Tyndale House Foundation. Used by permission of Tyndale House Publishers, Inc., Carol Stream, Illinois 60188. All rights reserved.

Scripture taken from The Message. Copyright © 1993, 1994, 1995, 1996, 2000, 2001, 2002. Used by permission of NavPress Publishing Group.

ISBN: 0-9979278-9-5
ISBN-13: 978-0-9979278-9-4

Every woman has the right and ability to be *happy*, *content*, and *fulfilled* as a single woman.

CONTENTS

INTRODUCTION

You did it! You made the decision to wait on God to send you the man of your dreams. You've dealt with so much heartbreak in your life and you've decided that you want better for yourself. Maybe you've spent your life watching other people search high and low, deep and wide for their spouses, only to end up with the wrong ones! Or, maybe you've been like the small handful of us who have spent the majority, if not all of our lives as single women, waiting for just the right man to come along at just the right time. Whatever situation you've been in and whatever you had to go through that brought you to who you are right now, you made it! And, let's face it…we all kind of suck at choosing a partner, and that's why we've decided to give God complete control over our future. And if you haven't, keep reading. You just might change your mind.

All too often, single women feel like they have to put on the face of false happiness when they are single, not being honest about, or maybe not even realizing that their period of "waiting" is not as pleasant as others make it seem. I, for one, spent a lot of years pretending to be happy, but only those closest to me knew that I was *really* unhappy with being single. And, at times I would even talk myself into being happy during certain times of year (read: Valentine's Day), attempting to avoid the sadness I really felt. It was easier to pretend than to actually deal with the real feelings, but we can only pretend for so long before people will begin to see the *real* us.

As we dig deep into revealing the truth about being single, waiting on God to bring someone into our lives, I will share with you my own experience with being single and not only becoming *satisfied* with not being married, but being happy with who I am as a single woman, whether I eventually get married or not. Yes, you read that right! We can be happy with our lives WHETHER WE GET MARRIED OR NOT. It sounds like such a hard pill to swallow, but trust me, by the end of this book, it will all be easier to understand, and for some (I hope all) to even accept and begin to live out.

Will becoming happy as a single person happen overnight? Perhaps. Only God knows what will happen for you and He is still in the miracle business, so something could quite possibly change for you overnight. Did it happen for me overnight? No. Was I *always* able to wake up in the morning, or go to bed at night with a smile on my face, knowing there was no man lying next to me? Absolutely not.

A lot of tears were shed.

A lot of questions were asked.

A lot of anger was let out.

A lot of journals have been filled in the process of me becoming completely satisfied with the fact that I am single with no husband-to-be in sight. Did I ever think that I could imagine myself not being married, with a smile on my face or the "woe is me" feeling? No. I actually thought the opposite would always be true. I thought that I would be unhappy until my Morris or Boris was waiting for me at the end of the aisle – that would be Chestnut and Kodjoe, for those who didn't catch it!

Getting to the place where I could truly be okay if no man ever asked me "Will you marry me?" was tough, but possible. Getting to the place where my desire is no longer for a man, but for God and only His plan for me was tough, but possible. I have learned that it *is* possible to be happy, even if marriage never happened for me. I have learned that *every woman has the right and ability to be happy, content, and fulfilled as a single woman*. Single ladies, YOU have the right to be happy, whether you're married or not!

Often times (okay, *most* times), single women, or people in general, pray for something and then hold God to a time slot to deliver. Even worse, we often receive a word from God and create a timeline of when we expect it to be fulfilled, becoming weary when our lives do not follow that timeline. Unfortunately, that time of waiting often becomes a heavy weight on our shoulders, robbing us of our strength and energy to do what God has called us to do, period.

When waiting on God, we are often completely consumed by thoughts of the thing we are waiting for. What we are waiting for takes over our conversations, wastes our mental energy, and even increases our imaginations [as we create completely made-up stories in our heads of how we want the situation to play out]! Waiting can be tiresome, stressful, nerve-racking, and a tense situation! Waiting sometimes causes us to worry, wonder, and do things that we would not do under normal circumstances, all because of this weight that we've put on our own shoulders to make sure something comes to pass. We then find ourselves in situations, relationships, or "situationships" hoping that those situations will lift that weight. This is all too true when waiting on God for a husband.

When God makes a promise, it is not our job to figure out how or when the promise will be fulfilled. It is our job to wait on God, put our expectation on Him that it will happen, and to continue pursuing His will for our lives. When we set a timeline on the promises of God and our prayers, we haven't set our expectations on God. We have, instead, set our expectations on time, which God doesn't operate in. Yes, maybe God made a promise to you about marriage or maybe you prayed for a husband. And yes, He will fulfill His promises. He's good for that. But, we must understand that although we may not see something happen within a certain time frame, it doesn't mean that it will not happen. It doesn't mean that God doesn't love you. It doesn't mean that you're undeserving of marital bliss. It doesn't mean you're not worthy. God always desires to bless us and He will never forget or forsake us.

If no one else will be honest enough to tell you, let me be the one: it is perfectly okay to realize that you are not happy being single, but it is *not* okay to stay in that place of being unhappy. By the end of this book, I hope that you will have learned one simple thing about waiting on God for marriage:

Do not allow your wait to become a weight.

1

THE WEIGHT OF WAITING

There are some people who receive a word from God and immediately see the manifestation of it. One minute they hear God speak something specific to their situation, they receive it in their hearts, and the next thing they know, God does exactly what He said He would do, exactly how He said He would do it. Praise God for that! And then there are those of us who hear a word from God, receive it in our hearts, and then find ourselves waiting months, years, or even decades before we see that promise from God come to fruition. We confess that promise from God, over and over in our daily devotions. We pray, "God, show yourself mighty!", "God, let your will be done!", and "God, I speak your promises into my life!", every single day, sometimes multiple times a day. And then...we wait some more. For some people, it appears to be easy for them to believe that God will do what they heard Him say, no matter how long it takes. They appear to be unwavering in their faith, and that is something to rejoice in! If that's you, I rejoice with you! But, if you're like me, chances are that *it has not been easy for you to have to wait to see things happen in your life*. And if you're reading *this* book, chances are *it has not been easy for you to have to wait to see things happen in your life*.

Can I let you in on a little secret? In both instances, either full of faith or lacking in the faith department, it takes the same faith of God to believe that His promises will come to pass. God's faith is God's faith. In the book of Romans, Paul says to *"be honest in your evaluation of yourselves, measuring yourselves by the faith God has given us"*, not by the *amount* of faith God has given us (Romans 12:3). We've all been given the same faith of God, but we have to use it. After having to wait for any amount of time, so many of us believe that if we do not see manifestation right away, then it either isn't going to happen for us, we don't deserve it, we didn't really hear from God, or the man of God who spoke the word to us was "prophelying". While any of these things *could* be true, a lot of the time they are not. There is almost always something else holding us back from seeing God's promises. That's another subject for another day.

When we lose focus on the fact that God spoke to us and that His word will not return back to Him void, all those months or years of waiting for things to happen become a heavy weight on our shoulders, weighing down our spirits, causing our faith in God to waiver, mentally stressing us out, causing us to gain weight (Oh Lord, no!), and sometimes causing physical strain on our bodies.

The weight of the wait sometimes costs us our freedom to live the lives that God designed us for. By this, I mean that we get so caught up in waiting for the next moment or the next thing, that we forget to *live*. Even worse, we allow sadness or depression to overcome us and we, sometimes literally, lock ourselves up in our rooms and never do anything. We never take time to discover what we like to do or take that dream vacation we've always wanted to take. We exert so much energy in daydreaming of the day we'll get to honeymoon with our husbands, that we never even consider that we could do those same things and go on those same vacations as single women...without the man, of course. Allowing our wait time to become a weight could cost us our happiness, if we are not careful. It could cost us our lives.

In those times when you feel like waiting on God is too difficult and you want to take matters into your own hands, do me a favor. Get a sheet of paper and a pen. Write down every reason that you can think of about why you do not want to wait. Now, pick up that sheet of paper and ball it up. Get up out of your chair and walk to the trashcan. Now, here is the best part! Throw that piece of trash into the trash! Literally, cast your cares into that trashcan. All of those reasons that you came up with about why you do not want to wait do not even come close in comparison to the joy that you will experience after the wait.

The word of God says to cast your cares upon God because He cares about everything that concerns you and that He will carry the weight of whatever troubles you. When things in our lives cause us to worry, to be stressed, to be fearful, and to doubt, God does not require that we work things out on our own. He wants to take care of us! He wants to work things out for us. He wants to be the answer to our questions! If we do not cast our cares onto God, we are literally choosing to carry the weight of them. We are choosing to worry and take on the responsibility of making decisions that could potentially harm us or keep us from living our best lives.

I like to think of the period of waiting this way: the longer you have to wait for your man, the better that man will be when he finds you and the better your marriage will be once he does! God is not going to give you just any man in any mental state. He's not going to send you just any old body. He's going to give you His best. I don't know about you, but I'd rather wait and allow God to shape that man into the best version of himself, while I'm spending time with God, allowing Him to shape me into the best version of myself.

Once I let go of the weight of my waiting period, I found myself smiling for no reason and asking myself if I was truly happy. I mean, I literally asked myself, "are you actually happy right now, knowing you're still single and could possibly be single forever?" It was almost unbelievable! And to be honest, it was so unbelievable that I almost believed the enemy when he said, "your joy isn't real and it will eventually fade away because no one is happy being single". Yeah, he said that. That old snot nose devil...

Remember that no matter how difficult the wait seems to be, don't allow the wait become a burden. The waiting period is the time when you decide who you're going to be and what kind of lifestyle you want to create for yourself. Waiting is good! Weight, not so much.

One of my favorite singers has a lyric in one of her songs that says this:

> *"You're not required to carry the weight. So, let it go. Here's my hand to hold. At the end of it all, there's a smile, for you, waiting. So, breathe in and let it go."* – Tori Kelly, *Something Beautiful*

Let go of the weight!

"Therefore, since we are surrounded by such a huge crowd of witnesses to the life of faith, let us strip off every weight that slows us down, especially the sin that so easily trips us up. And let us run with endurance the race God has set before us."

Hebrews 12:1 (NLT)

2

CHANGE THE WAY YOU WAIT

Before we get into what "waiting on God" means and how to change the way you wait, let's talk about what "waiting" does not mean. Waiting on God does not mean sitting in a chair, on the couch, on the bed, or walking down the street waiting for God to bring us something or for it to fall out of a tree like a piece of ripe fruit. Oh, that'll preach! Waiting on God does not mean that we pray that God will do something for us and then we sit and stare around the room, looking for it to fall from the ceiling. Waiting on God does not mean that we wait for God to bring someone or something into our lives and we have absolutely no action on our end. It does not mean that we sit paralyzed, as if we are unable to move our limbs when God says to move them, because we're "waiting". And ladies, waiting on God does not mean that you never even move your lips to speak to any man until God shows up in your room and tells you that such and such will be your man and then such and such magically knocks on your front door five minutes later, asking for your hand in marriage. Besides, God says to be brave and of good courage when we wait. There is nothing brave or courageous about sitting on the couch, eating potato chips, waiting for your knight in shining armor to knock down your front door. Just saying. Trust me, I've dreamt that dream, too, and it was just that...a dream.

Listen, if the scenario I just described happens to you, please contact me immediately so that we can share your testimony with the masses!

The word "wait" is generally defined this way: to stay where one is or delay action until a particular time or until something happens (google.com). While this is true in a general sense, this type of waiting is not the type of waiting that God wants us to do when we say that we are "waiting on God to bring me my husband". The type of waiting we should be doing can be described by the following definitions: 1) to act as a waiter or waitress, serving food and drink (google.com) and 2) to be available or in readiness (dictionary.reference.com).

Let's use our imaginations for a minute, shall we? Picture yourself at your favorite restaurant. You know, the one where you order the filet mignon and the best garlic mashed potatoes in town. Yeah, the one with the fresh baked bread sitting at the table when you get there. Or, if you're like me, you go to the place that has the freshest and most succulent...vegetables. Yes, vegetables! You know, the place where the asparagus is steamed just right and the spinach is sautéed with just the right amount of garlic and EVOO. And don't forget the steaming hot rolls with honey butter or the cake-like, melt-in-your-mouth skillet cornbread! Wait...is this a cookbook? I digress.

You get the picture. When the waiter comes to your table, he will generally (or should) introduce himself by such and such name and tell you what he will help you with throughout your visit. He'll ask what drinks you want to start with, tell you what the chef's special is for the night, and then give you a minute to look over the menu before you place your order. He'll usually give you about five to ten minutes to decide on an appetizer and then ask what you want to start your meal with. If you order an appetizer, he'll put that order in and come back to check on you. When he comes to check on you and/or bring your appetizer, he'll ask if you're ready to place an order for your main course. Throughout your meal, your waiter is the one who will check with you, periodically, to see if you need anything. He may refill your drink, bring condiments to the table, or provide any extra napkins or utensils you may need.

Now, imagine if your waiter came to your table, told you who he was and then sat down at a table next to yours, staring at you, but never came to take your order, never came to check on you to see if you needed him to do anything, and never did anything unless you asked him to. You'd be frustrated, right? You'd say he was doing a terrible job for someone who called himself a waiter. You may even say he is not doing his job at all and doesn't deserve to be on the payroll. You'd say that he is not taking any initiative and that he is literally *waiting for you* to do everything and doing absolutely nothing unless you ask him to. Imagine if after all of that and after finally finishing your meal, he had the nerve to ask for a tip! If you happened to have survived that meal without once complaining to the manager, the last thing you are thinking about is giving him a tip!

This is how we are, sometimes, when it comes to waiting on God. We tell God, "Okay, I'm here and I need this, so I'm just gonna sit here and wait for you to give it to me. I'm not going to put in any real effort to serve you, because I'm waiting for you to tell me what to do. So, if you need me, I'll be over here in this corner, not doing anything". That sounds funny, right? But, that is exactly what the waiter in the second scenario above is doing and I believe that is how we look to God sometimes when we call ourselves "waiting on Him". I bet you'd never eat at that restaurant again and I bet you'd tell everyone you knew to not eat there either.

Aren't you glad God is not like us?

Aren't you glad that God does not withhold His blessings and favor from us just because we haven't yet learned how to truly wait on Him? Aren't you glad that God is patient with us and does not complain to other people about our terrible "service"? Imagine if God complained to our pastors and leaders about how we serve Him. Imagine if God told your pastor, "This child is terrible. All I did was tell her to be an usher because the ushers needed help for a few months, and all she did was complain every single Sunday. She didn't even last an entire month! If she had just been obedient and did what I told her, she would have known that someone she seated was going to give her a $10,000 check two months later." Imagine if our blessings were dependent upon our obedience to God and how we serve Him.

The waiter who tends to you and anticipates your needs is fulfilling his job responsibilities as a waiter by making sure that your order is right, that it gets out to you on time and is still hot, and to provide for you anything you need during your meal. Although he may have other tables to tend to, he is always available and in readiness to serve. This is how we should be with God. We are to act as waiters or waitresses, always available, doing what He says, when He says to do it, and in readiness to serve Him whenever He needs us to do something. Even when we have other things ("tables", families, friends, jobs, and businesses) to tend to, it is our reasonable service to serve God in this way. Turn your waiting into serving.

Serving means to be of service to someone, to be attentive to the needs of another person, to be available and joyfully willing to provide help when someone is in need, and to do it with your whole heart! Other words for serve are provide, supply, operate, and work. When we "serve" God, are we providing His hands and feet in the earth? Are we using our gifts and talents as a supply for the body of Christ to use? Are we operating and working as unto the Lord? Be honest with yourself for a minute. Are you waiting the way that the Bible teaches us to wait? Are you truly serving God?

If we truly do a heart and mind check on ourselves, some of us may have answers that we may not want to admit to. Some of us may realize that we have not been of service to God and attentive to what He needs us to do when it comes to reaching out and impacting the lives of those around us. We may not have been honestly joyful about some of the things God has asked us to do. Okay, I'll speak for myself. Sometimes, I am not always thrilled about things God tells me to do and, sometimes, I've ignored those things. I'm not proud of it, obviously, but, you live and you learn, folks!

I encourage you to do a heart and mind check right now. Go and get another sheet of paper and write down some of the things that God has asked you to do and how you felt, good or indifferent, about doing those things. Write down whether or not you were happy to do what He asked and whether or not you were obedient. From your notes, you should be able to determine whether or not you were truly serving God and "waiting" on Him.

How we each serve God is different, because not everyone has the same set of spiritual gifts, talents, and passions. Not everyone is skilled in the same areas and not everyone has the ability to do everything. This is where your personal relationship with God comes in. You have to know God for yourself in order to know what He wants you to do. You have to know what He put inside of you in order to know what you should be doing for the kingdom and where you should be using your gifts. Most of all, you have to be confident in God so much that no matter what or who the enemy sends your way to distract you and throw you off your course, you can rest assured that you know your purpose and that what you're doing is exactly what God created you to do. This is how you serve.

"God has given each of you a gift from his great variety of spiritual gifts. Use them well to serve one another. Do you have the gift of speaking? Then speak as though God himself were speaking through you. Do you have the gift of helping others? Do it with all the strength and energy that God supplies. Then everything you do will bring glory to God through Jesus Christ. All glory and power to him forever and ever! Amen."

First Peter 4:10-11 (NLT)

3

WHY YOU SHOULD WAIT FOR GOD TO SEND YOUR HUSBAND

There are countless stories in the Bible of people becoming impatient in their waiting, taking matters into their own hands. We all know how that turns out. Not. So. Well.

Have you ever been in a situation where you thought you knew everything, and you made a decision based only on the information you had, and then something happened as a result of a piece of information you *did not* have, and it threw you completely off? I'm sure we all have, at least once or twice. What if you had known everything there was to know about that situation, so that you could have made a more informed decision? That would be awesome, right? Well, unfortunately, there is no way for us as humans to know everything there is to know about every situation, especially when it comes to dealing with other humans. But, that's why we serve an amazing God who knows all, who knows what's best for us, and who can and will guide us into making the best decisions for our lives, without us having to know everything there is to know about a situation, or person, in this case. Wouldn't it be awesome to meet and marry a guy who will be exactly what you need, without you even knowing it? The world would be a much better place if each of us were all-knowing and could make decisions based on all of that knowledge we had and everyone made perfect decisions because everyone knew everything. Wait! I'm not sure if everyone knowing everything would create a perfect world, but you know what I mean!

All throughout our lives, we make misinformed, partially-informed, or not-at-all-informed decisions, especially when we as women choose some of the men we allow into our lives. We choose to let "clowns" into our lives to play with our hearts because they are physically attractive. We allow grown boys into our lives to leach off of us because we think that we can groom them into the men we want them to be. We allow "bad boys" into our space because they provide a sense of protection for us, but we become upset when they do not express their feelings to us the way we want them to. We all know where these scenarios can potentially lead us.

Although we may think that Mr. Fine-as-the-day-is-long is the man we need, he may not be the man that God has for us, for whatever reasons. And some of those reasons may never be revealed to us, but they'll be exactly why we need to stay away from that man. While I do not want to scare you, let's put into practical terms some of the things you may find out *after* marrying the wrong guy:

1)   You want to start saving for a house in the suburbs as soon as you get married. He wants to live in his loft in the city for the rest of his life.

2)   You want to have at least three children. He already has two kids from a previous relationship and doesn't want any more.

3)   You want to travel the world with him for at least the first five years of your marriage. He's a homebody, who doesn't like to fly, and thinks vacationing is a waste of money.

4)   You are comfortable in your nine-to-five. He wants to build a legacy of wealth and wants you to help build a family business.

5)   You want him to warm up your car every morning and shovel it out of the snow during the winter...by himself...because

that's what your dad did for your mom. He thinks you should warm up your own car and help him shovel the snow.

6) You do not like to cook and have mastered the art of ordering out. He prefers home cooked meals and thinks you should cook breakfast, lunch, and dinner every day of the week. Yeah, even in this day and time.

7) You want to climb the corporate ladder before you have children, and couldn't see yourself sitting at home doing nothing all day long. He doesn't want you to work and wants to take care of your needs.

Or even some worse case scenarios:

1) You have been debt free for the past five years and you find out two months into your marriage that he has a gambling problem and owes $10,000 to a loan shark.

2) He told you that he has never been married and you find out only a year into your marriage that he not only has an ex-wife, but he also has three kids with her and she's full of drama.

I think that's enough.

While no marriage or relationship situation will be perfect, and you will have to seriously discuss some things and come to several mutual agreements, you have to recognize, for your own sanity and well-being, that there are some things that you will not be willing to compromise on, in order preserve the quality of life that you want to live. And listen, if you do not ask God to help you, to help your husband-to-be find you, and to reveal certain things about that man, you're at risk of marrying the wrong man and living unhappily ever after. Nobody wants to wait 25+ years to end up married to someone who is difficult to get along with and who they cannot build a solid future with. That would be a disaster.

I remember a time when I was introduced to a young man who the person who introduced us thought would be great for me. We began talking, and for a short while he did seem to be perfect, but there was something off about him. When we first began talking to each other on the phone, he would tell me about all the great mentoring opportunities he's had and how he would teach his nieces and nephews various Bible stories. He had me in awe as I listened intently to what he shared with me. As he recalled the times that he taught those Bible stories, it was as if, in that very moment, he were teaching me. During that same conversation, I was laying on my bed, holding the phone to my ear, listening. Suddenly, I heard God speak to me almost as if He were laying right there next to me. God said to me, "he's not the one". I said to God, "but, he's perfect!". God said back to me, "but, he's not the one". Let me tell you that immediately after I heard that and every time I thought about him or saw his name light up the screen on my cell phone, my stomach turned. My spirit was so uneasy, having heard clearly that this man was not "the one" for me, yet, I still entertained him for a short time after that.

We texted every day, throughout the day. He would call me after his basketball games and he'd tell me how the games went. Everything was going great. However, knowing what I knew, I struggled with how I would get out of what *seemed* like the perfect situation, without having to tell him what God had said to me. I was confused that God would speak so clearly against the relationship, but hadn't immediately given me a way out. I prayed, "Lord, please show me how to get out of this" because I was literally sick to my stomach every time I spoke to this guy. I had no idea how I would get out of it, but I knew I had to. One day not too long after, it all went downhill. Long story short, after about a month and a half of talking on the phone and texting back and forth, we had a pointless argument over something so very small, and ended up never talking to or seeing each other again. In the moment when I felt like I was drowning, God sent a lifeboat!

While I do not know to this day why a man who seemed so perfect for me was not *the one* for me, I am so grateful that not only did God tell me that he wasn't the one, but that God provided a way of escape before anyone had the chance to be hurt. God has not always spoken that clearly to me regarding the small handful of men who came into my life, probably because I knew better and didn't need to be told that *such and such* was not worthy of my time. But, this time was different. I knew that God had to tell me "NO" to this man because he *appeared* to be perfect and I could have easily fallen for him, eventually.

"Therefore judge nothing before the time, until the Lord come, who both will bring to light the hidden things of darkness, and will make manifest the counsels of the hearts: and then shall every man have praise of God." First Corinthians 4:5 (KJV)

Thank God for the lifeboat!

Most of all, I'm so grateful that in God telling me that he was not the one, I could rest assured that there *is* one.

In reflecting on that moment in my life, I came to realize that I do not have to worry about whether or not someone is right for me. I know that if God would save me from drowning in that situation, that He will also save me from drowning in every other situation by telling me "he's not the one" and that He will lead me into the best relationship for me by telling me "this man *is* the one".

If we make life, relationship, and marriage decisions based only on our feelings and what we think we know, we set ourselves up for failure. We do not know everything there is to know about every man who pursues or approaches us. It isn't physically or mentally possible for that to happen. This is why we need God! We need God to reveal things about those men so that we do not entertain the wrong ones. We need God to reveal things about ourselves, so that we know what kind of man we'll really need in order to be happy. We need God to tell us "no" when we want to date someone that we shouldn't. And, ladies, we need God to tell us "yes" when the time is right.

Waiting for God to send you a husband is vital to the success of your marriage and your future. Only God knows who is best for you. Only God knows who you'll be compatible with. Only God knows who has your best interest in mind and who genuinely loves you like Christ loves the church. And for a select few of us (we know who we are), only God knows who can put up with us and ALL of our amazingness! Only God is all-knowing, so let Him do it. Besides, allowing God to do all the work in shaping that man into the man he should be takes the pressure off of you. All you have to do is wait for him to come around and listen for God to say YES!

"Why would you ever complain, O Jacob, or whine, Israel, saying, 'God has lost track of me. He doesn't care what happens to me'? Don't you know anything? Haven't you been listening? God doesn't come and go. God lasts. He's Creator of all you can see or imagine. He doesn't get tired out, doesn't pause to catch his breath. And he knows everything, inside and out. He energizes those who get tired, gives fresh strength to dropouts. For even young people tire and drop out, young folk in their prime stumble and fall. But those who wait upon God get fresh strength. They spread their wings and soar like eagles, they run and don't get tired, they walk and don't lag behind."

Isaiah 40:27–31 (MSG)

4

HOW TO WAIT WHEN YOU HAVE A PROMISE FROM GOD

A lot of us have heard from one prophet, minister, pastor, leader or another, these words: "your husband is coming". Let's just get one thing straight. Be careful who you allow to speak into your life. Be very careful who you allow to plant seeds. Always, always, always hear God for yourself!

There are a lot of false prophets who may know or think they know a little about you or your life, and may "feel in their spirit" that God told them to tell you something. While that statement could be true coming from true prophets, it isn't *always* God telling someone to say those things, per se.

How do you make sure that someone is truly hearing from God? Try the spirit in them by Holy Spirit inside of you! If it doesn't seem right, it probably is not. If what they said is contrary to what you know God told you, that person did not hear from God. If what they said contradicts the word of God (the Bible), that person did not hear from God. Point blank and the period.

Over the years, many people have said things to me like, "You've been holding on, sister. Your husband is coming soon" or "Don't worry, your husband is coming" or "Keep doing what you're doing, God is preparing your husband for you", or my favorite, "You're going to marry a pastor". While these things could very well be true, they may not have necessarily been rhema words or a prophecy, as the people who said those things would like to say that they were. I find it funny when people take a general encouraging statement that could be for any single woman of marriage-ready age, and speak it to me as if God said to them, "Nicole needs to hear this. Go and tell her this, right now!" I believe that if God will tell someone who I do not know from the next person, to speak a specific word or prophecy to me, that word or prophecy will not only reveal something that they could not have known outside of me telling them, it will be confirmation of what God already revealed to me it, and/or an answer to an issue or question that I had at that particular time in my life. If none of those is true, please keep it moving.

I am generally not a person who desires things and would not take those desires to God. If there is something going on in my life, 9 times out of 10, I am going to pray about it at least once. On one particular Sunday morning during praise and worship, I was in church and someone came to me and said, "You have not because you ask not".

Crickets.

I looked this individual in the eyes, with genuine confusion, as I said to myself, "that's random". Why was it random and why was I confused? Because there was nothing going on in my life at the time that I felt like I should not pray for. There was nothing on my mind in that moment that I desired. There was nothing that lined up with what this person had said. There was nothing said that did not directly deal with something that had happened to me or that I was thinking about. Had I been in the mood to argue or to prove a point, I probably would have said something like this:

> *"What are you talking about? You don't even know me and that's random. This is the third time you have spoken to me about something that had nothing to do with me, that never came to pass. I need you to go back into your prayer closet and try again."*

But, I was in church, so what did I do? I simply said, "okay" and went back to singing along with the praise team.

On a completely different occasion, there was a particular moment in my life when I felt like no one cared anything about me or what I was doing. I felt like I was so alone in my walk with God and in life, in general, and that God had neglected me. One day when I was at church, someone came over to me and gave me a hug and spoke something to me that was so clear that I could not deny it. She said to me, "God loves you so much and you are so special to Him. He hasn't forgotten about you and He is going to bless everything that you've worked so diligently on". Now that, ladies, was an on time word of encouragement.

The moral of the story is that when someone speaks or tries to speak into your life, make sure that what they are saying aligns with God's word that is either written in the Bible or that God spoke to you. Make sure that it is not only true to your situation, but that it is also profitable and beneficial to your life.

"Don't suppress the Spirit, and don't stifle those who have a word from the Master. On the other hand, don't be gullible. Check out everything, and keep only what's good. Throw out anything tainted with evil." 1 Thessalonians 5:19-22 (MSG)

Whether or not you have seen the promise you had from God right away or still have yet to see it, remember that God is not bound by our clocks or our impatience. What God is bound by is His own word. Just because we feel that five years is long enough for us to wait for a husband, that doesn't mean that God is obligated to bring us a husband at the end of five years. Unless God specifically told you in 2010 that you would be married five years from that time, then you should not be surprised that you are still single in 2016.

You all know the woman in the Bible who suffered from

chronic bleeding. She suffered for twelve years before she was healed by touching Jesus' clothes (Luke 8:43-48). Jacob worked for Leah and Rachel's father for fourteen years until he was able to take Rachel as his wife (Genesis 29). Am I saying that you'll be forced to wait twelve, fourteen or even twenty years before you receive a promise from God? No, I am not saying that, but I am also not saying that you will not have to wait. I am not God so I cannot tell you how soon or not so soon He will manifest His promise or an answered prayer to you.

What I am saying is that in both situations, those individuals held onto the promises and faith they had to receive something that they waited years to receive. In the case of the woman with the issue of blood, we do not even know how long she had been praying for healing. In the case of Jacob and Rachel, we do not know how long, if at all, Jacob had been looking for a wife before he saw Rachel tending to the sheep and knew instantly that he wanted her. All we know is what the Bible tells us about these situations. So, what I am trying to convey here is that we do not know how long we will have to wait and believe and renew our minds before we receive a husband as an answer to a prayer we've prayed. No one knows how long someone else has been praying for something that happened for them and no one knows what the next person has dealt with, sacrificed, or changed in order to receive a blessing.

When you know beyond a shadow of a doubt that God spoke to you either audibly, through His word, or through a true prophet, it is vital that you always remember *your* promise from God, even when everything around you looks like it is the opposite of what God said. Even when everything around you seems to point in the opposite direction of God's promise to you, remember God. Remember what He has done in the past. Remember that He is faithful to fulfill every promise He makes and that He does not break His promises like man does. God doesn't lie and He makes good on His word (Numbers 23:19).

"If God gives such attention to the appearance of wildflowers — most of which are never even seen — don't you think he'll attend to you, take pride in you, do his best for you? What I'm trying to do here is to get you to relax, to not be so preoccupied with getting, so you can respond to God's giving. People who don't know God and the way he works fuss over these things, but you know both God and how he works. Steep your life in God-reality, God-initiative, God-provisions. Don't worry about missing out. You'll find all your everyday human concerns will be met."

Matthew 6:30-33 (MSG)

5

WHAT DO YOU HAVE TO OFFER?

If you've followed my blog for any amount of time, you know that I am all about teaching and inspiring women to pursue God, pursue their passions, and to find their purpose in the world. In one of my blog posts, I wrote about one of my favorite speakers and wealth builders who spoke about finding and *being* a purpose partner. She spoke about how women spend so much time looking for a man, that they never discover their own purpose and end up in various relationships, having nothing to offer the relationship. She challenged listeners to ask themselves this one thing: *"how can we expect God to send us a purpose partner if we are not even living in our purpose?"*

I was speechless. Not only was it a thought provoking question, it opened my eyes even more to what God has instructed me to teach. It is far too common that women wait until marriage to live fully their lives. Far too often, we believe that our lives do not begin until we walk down the aisle. While I do believe that married life could be some of the best years of your life, it should not be the beginning of your life and certainly not the only part of your life.

Most of us have a desire to be married to this perfect man of God who has everything we have ever wanted in a man and does everything we've ever wanted our husbands to do and he is just perfect and makes our every dream come true. News flash! How can we expect him to be perfect if we are not perfect? And to my point, how can we expect him to have so much to offer the relationship if *we* have absolutely nothing to offer the relationship. It isn't fair and it isn't a recipe for success.

We women tend to focus on all the wrong things when it comes to preparing for marriage. Sure, we should definitely work on becoming physically healthier, getting our bodies in the best shape and saving money for the wedding. But, what happens after this man finds you and you walk down the aisle and come back from honeymooning in Jamaica? Will you be able to pray for him if he is sick? Will you be able to encourage him and make financial moves if he loses his job or decides to leave his job with nothing lined up? Will you be able to speak the word of God to him when he feels discouraged or faces a trial in his life that challenges his faith? Will you be there to intercede for him? Will you be able to help him make decisions about dreams he wants to achieve? Will you have *anything* to offer?

If you are only focused on your husband and what he has going on, what happens when he's out of town? What happens when he goes away for a two-week business trip? What happens if his job moves him across the country, or the world, for months at a time? When he is out making moves, you'll be sitting at home playing in your hair and eating a bag of potato chips, waiting for him to get back. While he's away fulfilling his purpose and doing ministry, you'll be at home wishing you had a hobby or a purpose of your own to fulfil.

Instead of us spending all of our single lives asking God, "when is my husband coming?" or "when are you going to send my man of God?", we should be asking Him, "where do I belong in your kingdom?" and "who can I encourage to go after their dreams?". Believe it or not, you have a purpose! You are not breathing for no reason. There is something inside of you that you love to do and that you could certainly do for the kingdom of God, no matter what it is. Your purpose fulfils a purpose for God.

The second, and maybe most important part of finding your purpose is making sure that the man you desire is headed in the same direction that you are headed in. There is nothing worse than connecting with a man you are attracted to, only to find out that he does not have the same or a similar vision for his life. For example, let's say "Morris" is just the right height, drives the car that you've always wanted, owns a home in a great neighborhood, and doesn't have any kids yet. He is perfect. But, you quickly get to know him and eventually learn that God has called him to travel and do missions work for the rest of his life. On the other hand, God has called you to mentorship in your local church. If you end up marrying "Morris", your relationship is sure to be strained, *if* it survives. Neither of you will be truly happy in that marriage because your purposes do not align.

There is absolutely nothing wrong with him taking frequent missions trips and there is absolutely nothing wrong with you spending much of your time mentoring kids, locally. The problem in this type of situation is that he'll be away most of time and won't be able to do ministry with you or spend much time with you. In addition, you'll have a hard time scheduling time to travel because you have recurring local commitments. Granted, with a lot of communication and very hard work, this type of situation could *possibly* work out. There are exceptions to everything. But, I strongly believe that two people who are divinely connected by God to each other will have similar visions for their lives and will actually want to spend most of their time together. Truth be told, your marriage is more about the impact that you can make as a unit than it is about you and him cuddling and buying a house together.

Over the years, I've seen all types of marriages, some good and some not so good. Some of the best marriages I've witnessed are the ones where both the man and woman have the same heart for God's people and they serve in ministry together. Of course they may have things that one or the other may do separately from the other, but they almost always function better as a unit when they willingly serve together.

For practical purposes (you know how this goes by now), let's look at one of the simplest examples of a couple doing ministry together: When God calls you to a particular local church home, He is not going to tell your spouse to go somewhere else. (Mark 3:25)

Is the ministry that a couple does together exclusive to what they do inside the church building? Absolutely not. Ministry is not exclusive to the church building and is more often than not, done outside of the church building. While I do not want to get into a discussion about ministry outside the church walls, because that isn't what this book is about, I would like to offer a few examples of how married couples do ministry together.

1) If both are called to the marketplace, they could be in business together

2) If she's a singer, he may be her drummer or manager

3) They may have a heart to reach the homeless, so they visit homeless shelters and teach them how to get their lives back in order

4) They may have a heart for teaching people financial freedom, so they travel and speak about money at different men's and women's conferences

5) He may be a mentor to young boys in foster care and she loves to host gatherings for the kids at their home

6) She may be inspired to start a graphic t-shirt clothing line, and he's a graphic designer

You get the point.

There are so many ways that couples can do ministry together, outside of them being on the usher board or on the praise team together. By the way, if God tells you and your future hubs to be ushers, please be obedient! I have nothing against ushers or the usher board, for the record!

Take a look at some of the handful of celebrity couples that are spreading the message of purity in their relationships and "hands off" before marriage. I believe that they are serving God by publicly doing relationships God's way, by abstaining from sex before marriage. If you take a look at their testimonies before they met each other, you'll learn that, individually, God led them down that path of purity at some point before they even began dating. They each pursued God's purpose for their lives, and because they knew there was a better end waiting for them, they were obedient and eventually led to each other. Their ministry is the example they are setting for those who may find themselves in the same situation or just needing a reminder that holiness is still right! Because they know their purpose and allowed their purpose to lead them to each other and into ministry, these couples are literally doing ministry together.

It is important for us to know our purpose as individuals before God sends us a "purpose partner" because in order for our purpose to connect with our purpose partner, we have to be living in our purpose. And how will you know if someone is your purpose partner if you do not know what *your* purpose is? How will you know that he has the same vision? How will you know that his heart is for the things of God? How will you know that his purpose aligns with your purpose? You'll only know if you are walking in your own purpose.

If and when the day comes that we are divinely connected to

our purpose partner, we want to have something to offer him and the relationship. We want to know that we are contributing to the success of the marriage and to the success of each other. We want to know that we have something productive to do while the hubs is out of town. We also want to know that the hubs has something productive to do when *we* are out of town.

It's time to grab another sheet of paper! I guess I should have told you in the beginning that you'd need a notebook and a pen while you're reading! Ask God this one question: *Will you reveal my purpose to me and show me how to live it out?*

Everything that God tells you in that moment, write it down. No matter how big or small, write it down. Keep writing. All the ideas you had from years ago, write them down. That crazy idea you had about changing the world, write it down. Don't stop writing until God stops speaking. Go ahead and ask Him. He is patiently waiting for you to ask Him how you can serve Him.

"A worthy wife is a crown for her husband, but a disgraceful woman is like cancer in his bones."

Proverbs 12:4 (NLT)

6

HOW TO BE A "SATISFIED SINGLE"

In the past, every time I heard a woman say that she was a "satisfied single" woman, I just knew she was lying. I would think to myself, "how could you possibly be happy with not having a man in your life?" I asked myself, "is this woman just trying to hide the fact that she is sad that no man has asked to marry her?" I literally thought that any woman who said she was happy in her singleness was lying through her teeth…until I became one of those women.

I remember a particular moment when I was alone in my room and what I felt in that moment. I sat there, all alone, smiling for no particular reason at all. I was literally giggling to myself, out of the blue. Immediately, it hit me! I thought to myself, "Am I really happy even though I don't have a husband or a man, at all? Am I really sitting here, smiling for reason, and I am still single?" Those thoughts took me to a place I had never been before. "Will I truly be happy if I *never* get married?" I asked myself.

As I sat there, all alone, and the answer to those questions was a huge YES, all of heaven rejoiced! Well, I don't know if it happened *quite* like that, but I like to think the angels threw a party for me, in celebration of the fact that I no longer felt like I needed a husband to complete my life. I like to think that God said to the angels, "That's my girl! Her only desire is ME now!" I like to think that heaven rejoiced because I was no longer feeling depressed, down-trodden, and lonely in the reality that I was single in my thirties and almost everyone around me was married. I was no longer a *sorry* single, but I had finally regained my freedom to live because I had become a *satisfied* single.

You may be asking, "if you're truly a satisfied single, then why do you always talk about singleness?" I'll answer that gladly, but just know that singleness is not the only facet of who I am, just as marriage should not be the only facet of who I am. I have many other interests, but this book is not about my other interests, and my ministry to single women is not about my other interests.

Why do I talk about singleness?

1) I have never been married, so I cannot talk about that. Singleness is all I have ever known.

2) God has freed me from the bitterness of being single and has lifted the weight of the wait to be married. He has commissioned me to share that freedom with you! I spent so many nights (why do we always say "many nights" as if these things do not happen in the daytime?) wondering when God was going to send me a husband. I asked God what was wrong with me, that I was in my late twenties and early thirties and still single. I was angry with God for blessing everyone else with a husband and here I was still single and nowhere near being married. I was frustrated every night and day. But thanks be to God! He has carried away the weight!

I can and do talk about singleness as a satisfied single because I want for you, married or single, to know and love yourself outside of your husband or husband-to-be. I talk about singleness because I want so badly for you, too, to be able to sit on the edge of your bed, all alone, and say with a big fat YES that if you never get married, you will not just be satisfied with your life, but that you'll be happy! The only way to achieve that is to know God, pursue and fulfill your purpose and passion in life, and live!

Was it a breeze, going from saved, single, and sad, to where I am today? Oh, please! Not at all. It was difficult…really difficult and almost impossible, or so I thought.

How did I get there?

After years of journaling, writing, and singing the same sad songs of my lonely, single life, I decided that enough was enough and discovered that my mind and heart would not change unless *I* changed. My desire would not magically change toward God out of the blue. I had to work for it. I had to seek God and allow Him and His word to be my desire. I had to allow God to show me how to use my gifts to bring about change around me and to bring about change into my own life.

As simple as it may sound, it all began with me reading the Bible. Yep, simple as that. Of course I had read the Bible many times before this period in my life, but I was reading more out of a feeling of obligation than an actual need. I realized that if I wanted peace of mind and true joy, I *needed* the word of God to be inside of me. I needed to understand God's word outside of what I had learned on Sunday mornings and Wednesday nights.

God's word became my medicine. It became my teacher. It became the way that I could understand why certain things happened and it helped me understand and know God better. And at times, the word became my outlet when I wanted someone to talk to. When I wanted a husband to tell me he loved me, God told me that He loved me through His word. In those times when I wanted to daydream about being on my honeymoon, I allowed the word of God to fill my thought life. And, in those tough times when I wanted someone to encourage me, God reminded me that He created me to do great things and that He had my back! God showed me that He had an answer to every problem I had. Most of all, the word of God reminded me of my purpose.

Ladies, it is indeed possible for you, too, to get to the place where you only desire the things of God. You must come to the place where you know that God has your best life set up for you, but you have to trust Him to show you the way to it, even if that means letting go of your desire to be married right away. If your desire to be married is the only thing you think about, it could cost you your happiness.

Getting started on this amazing journey of freedom:

Set your eyes, thoughts, and life on heavenly things.

Colossians 3:1-18 talks about "thinking about heavenly things, not things of earth" and what that looks like in reality. When Christ died, we died with Him. And when He arose, we arose with Him. When we receive new life through Christ's resurrection, our real life is in Christ, not in the old life we had without Him. Without God, we sought after our own desires and pleasing our flesh with men and/or earthly things. Our feelings and affection were literally set on how men made us feel by what they did, said, or gave us.

Have you ever been secretly in love with someone and found out that he either did not like you the same way or that he liked someone else? What did that do to your self-esteem? Yeah, those are the feelings I'm talking about. What happened when you found out that he didn't like you? Most of us immediately became sad, depressed, and felt like we were not good enough for him to like us. Just like a thermostat is set on a certain temperature and the room adjusts based on what the thermostat says, we were set on that man and our feelings adjusted based on what he said. That was the old way of thinking in the old life.

With this new life – this new life in Christ – we have a new way of thinking, a pure way of living, and our affection is set on God, not on man. We now can live a life of freedom, knowing that no matter how short or tall we are, not matter how short or long our hair is, no matter how educated or uneducated we are, God will always love us and He will always choose us.

Stop comparing your life to other people's lives.

Live your own life! Galatians 6:4-5 is plain and simple. It reads: *"Pay careful attention to your own work, for then you will get the satisfaction of a job well done, and you won't need to compare yourself to anyone else. For we are each responsible for our own conduct."* (NLT)

It goes without saying that you never know what someone is really dealing with just by looking at them. Unless someone has shared their entire life experiences with you, you never know how difficult their relationships are or have been. Everyone is different. Everyone has a different purpose. Everyone goes through different learning experiences. Everyone has a different personality and what they will be willing to deal with. I realized not long ago that comparing myself to other people and not loving myself was an insult to God, as if to say that what He created was not good enough.

Honestly, ladies…if God brought a man into your life today, would you really be ready to deal with everything that comes with him and that relationship? There's a time and place for every single thing that happens in your life. And listen, it is okay to want him to come, but you also want to be ready when he does.

Choose joy.

In Philippians 4:4, Paul tells us to rejoice in the Lord. If joy was unending, he would not have told us to *re*-joice. If joy lasted forever without any effort, we would not have to choose it every day! Paul literally tells us to have joy over and over and over again!

Redo joy! Even in the rough times, we can choose to have joy. Even when our friends let us down, we can choose joy. Even if we're single, we can have joy! We choose joy by deciding to be thankful for what we have and where we are, not focusing on what we DO NOT have or what we HAVE NOT done yet. It is, indeed, much easier said than done, but it can be done. It's a choice.

Pursue your passion and live your God-given life.

Whatever you do, do it well…the Bible says so! No, really, God tells us to be diligent and persistent in our work. And honestly, there is no point in having interest in something if we are not going to do it and there is no point in doing something if we are not going to go all out! God gave you life. Be passionate about it!

"You're blessed when you're content with just who you are – no more, no less. That's the moment you find yourselves proud owners of everything that can't be bought. You're blessed when you've worked up a good appetite for God. He's food and drink in the best meal you'll ever eat. You're blessed when you care. At the moment of being "carefull", you find yourselves cared for. You're blessed when you get your inside world – your mind and heart – put right. Then you can see God in the outside world."

Matthew 5:5-8 (MSG)

CLOSING

Without a husband, you are still a child of God. Without a husband, you still have purpose. Without a husband, you still have a plan to fulfill. Without a husband, you can still serve God. Without a husband, you're still passionate about things. Without a husband, you still have things that you want to do. Without a husband, God still has things for you to do. Without a husband, you can still be happy and you can still find joy in life.

It is my hope that you have learned how to embrace your period of waiting and to not allow it to become a weight on your shoulders. I sincerely pray that you have been encouraged to continue your journey to discovering your passion, or that you have at least decided to begin. It is my heart's desire that you, single or married, literally DIS-COVER your purpose, meaning there is no longer a cover over your purpose in God and in the body of Christ.

My greatest desire as you live your life is that you will begin to realize that you have so much to offer this world, no matter what you've been through or may be going through right now. Let go of anything that has weighed you down during your waiting period and cast all of those cares and worries onto God. He is the one who cares for you and He is the only one who can bring you joy.

Ladies, it is perfectly okay to desire being married. But, it is not okay when your *only* desire is being married, causing you to neglect your relationship with God and neglect your own life. If you have dreams of vacationing in Paris, don't wait until your husband can go with you. Go now! (That's what I plan to do) If you've never been on a cruise, don't wait until you have someone to cuddle with in that tiny room. Go now! If you want to go skiing, go now! If you want to start a business, start it now! Whatever it is that you are able to do before you marry, don't hold off on those things until marriage. Do not allow yourself to miss out on so many great adventures because you're waiting for *him* to come. He may not come for another ten years and you will have wasted so much time.

And do not be like so many women who have not yet grasped the concept of satisfaction in who they are, individually. I was one of those women who thought it was not possible to be single and satisfied with who I am as a person, and I thought it would never happen for me. I was one of those women who was skeptical of other women who said they were satisfied singles, yet, I was a little envious of them. I wanted so badly to be able to say that I was "saved, single, and satisfied", and now I can! And I want you to be able to say it, too.

Now is the time to make a change. Now is the time to work on becoming the best you that you can be. Now is the time for you to begin walking out your purpose and holding nothing back! Now is the time to start serving God with your whole heart and rejoicing in how you can be of service in the body of Christ. Now is the time to turn your waiting into serving. Now is the time to shift your focus from looking for a purpose partner to *becoming* a purpose partner. Now is the time for you to become so amazing, so whole, so free, and so beautiful inside and out, that when your husband comes along, he will have no choice but to snatch you up, girl! There will be absolutely no way that he'll miss his blessing (you) because you'll be so wrapped up in the beauty of your purpose and he'll recognize that your purpose aligns with his. If you learn nothing else after reading this book, I pray that you learn this:

Wait with *trust*. Wait with *passion*. Wait with *service*. Wat with *purpose*.

Let go of the weight.

"...If it seems slow in coming, wait. It's on its way. It will come right on time."

Habakkuk 2:3 (MSG)

ABOUT THE AUTHOR

Nicole C. Diggs, author of When the Wait Becomes a Weight, spreads the message of pursuing purpose and passion before marriage through women's empowerment groups, books, her blog, and by sharing her real-life experience with many topics that people often are too afraid to discuss. It is her vision that people will begin to experience freedom in those areas of their lives by first being honest with who and where they are, and by asking and answering the hard questions.

As a serial entrepreneur, outside of working on her next big project, Nicole loves to travel and enjoy independent films in her free time. From songwriting to journaling to her very first novella, *The Waiting Game*, Nicole has always preferred written words as her avenue of expression.

19640556R00034

Printed in Great Britain
by Amazon